STRESS-FREE POTTY TRAINING

A Right Approach Guide for First-Time Parents.

by Immaculate Newsted

STRESS-FREE POTTY-TRAINING

A Right Approach Guide for First–Time Parents.

For information address:
J2B Publishing LLC
4251 Columbia Park Road
Pomfret, MD 20657
www.J2BLLC.com

This book is set in Garamond.
ISBN: 978-1-954682-55-9

STRESS-FREE POTTY TRAINING

A Right Approach Guide for First-Time Parents.

IMMACULATE NEWSTED

CONTENTS PAGE

Ch 1. Introduction: What is Considered "Successful" Toilet Learning?

A lot of information is available about toilet learning, and it can be overwhelming, especially if you're not sure where to begin or what will work best for your child.

Successful toilet learning involves the ability to go to the bathroom in a way that is comfortable and enjoyable for your child. It may not happen instantly, but once you get there, the rest will happen easily.

You don't have to be perfect at toilet learning. There are many different ways to successfully train your child and make it fun for them!

- Success means that the child is able to hold his or her pee or poo in until they're ready to go.

- If your child is able to go on the potty without any help from you and feels proud of it, then you have succeeded.
- If your child has been using the potty for a long time and you can't tell them any more stories or read a book with them.

If you're going to be successful at toilet teaching your child, you'll need to make a few things clear. First, you need to be clear about your expectations for the process. Do you think your child will learn how to use the potty in a day or two? Or do you think it'll take more time? Then, sit down with your child and talk about what they can expect from you during this time period. Are there any specific behaviors that are unacceptable while they are learning? You also need to be prepared for hard work, toilet learning isn't easy; it takes patience, consistency, and persistence on both sides of the equation.

Toilet Learning

Toilet learning is a major accomplishment of early childhood from both parent and child perspectives. You may notice that I chose to use the term *toilet learning* instead of *potty training* because I believe toileting is a skill that children should learn on their own and in their own time. Our only job as adults is to facilitate once we recognize readiness signs. As adults, we should look at toilet learning as a developmental milestone like learning to crawl, walk, feed oneself, jump, ride a wheeled toy, and perform any other small motor skills.

Some adults attach a great deal of significance to early "potty training." They may brag that they have "trained" their child at 18 months or even earlier than that. In these cases, it was actually not the child but the adult, who was trained. The adult was prepared to put the child at the right time at the child's proper bowel movement at regular intervals.

The child did not learn anything positive. This kind of training can be harmful to the child in the long run, as it does not involve a child's choosing or cooperation. What the child learns from this approach is that an adult expects him to do something that is totally beyond his capacity.

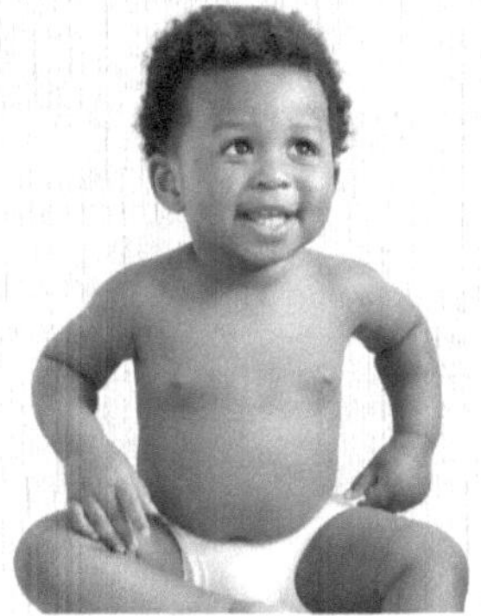

Parents with young children may feel tired of the diapering season. It might seem to them as if they are failing if they do not have their child toilet trained at a certain age. You should know that slow toilet learning does not reflect your child's intelligence or ability to achieve in other areas of life.

It is, therefore, important for you as a parent to relax and pay attention to your child's readiness to learn toileting on his or her own. Some preschools and daycare centers require that a child is able to go potty on his or her own.

Ch. 2. Recognizing Readiness and the Importance of Timing

Readiness is the key to successful toilet learning. There are so many signs that may tell that a child is ready for toilet learning. These signs include:

- The child stops playing while pooping or peeing.
- The child is very aware of his/her need to pee or have a bowel movement before the process occurs.
- The child stays dry for an hour or two at a time during the day and sometimes wakes up dry from naps.
- The child appears to be aware of what's going on during urinating or defecating process.
- The child's bowel movement schedule is fairly regular.
- The child understands the difference between wet and dry, and clean and dirty.
- The child is uncomfortable in a dirty diaper and asks to be changed.
- The child is interested in wearing underwear instead of diapers.

- The child can communicate her needs.
- The child can help dress and undress himself.
- The child can follow simple directions.
- The child can seat herself on a low potty chair or can climb a stool to seat on a toilet with a potty seat without an adult's help.
- The child can walk to the bathroom on her own.
- The child is interested in imitating what older children do.
- The child knows toilet words like poop or pee.

These signs and many more indicate that a child is ready for toilet learning. We should remember that a child has both the physiological ability to control her bladder and bowels and be psychologically ready before we start toilet learning.

What are Physiological and Psychological Readiness for Toilet Learning?

Success in toilet learning depends on timing! By timing, I mean physiological and psychological, not necessarily a certain age. A child might hear or even understand what you are saying but not have the capacity yet to carry out what you ask of her. Some children might be ready before turning two years old, some before three years old, and some after turning three years old.

As with other developmental milestones, each child is different. It is an adult's responsibility to understand each child's needs and capabilities and to support the child to meet those needs.

What Is Physiological Readiness?

The steady development of a child's gross and fine motor skills will help her to hold her clothes more effectively. This skill develops around 18 months of age. The skill will help the child engage in activities that might keep him seated on the potty long enough to successfully relieve himself.

Physiologically, the nerves and muscles that control bowels and bladders do not mature until 18 to 24 months. This means that the later a child starts toilet learning, the faster she will achieve bladder and bowel control.

In addition, children ready for toilet learning will usually have some control over their bladder and bowel movements.

Timing is important when it comes to toilet learning readiness. Forcing a child to toilet learn before he is ready can result in frustration and setbacks. Conversely, waiting too long to start toilet learning can make the process more difficult. Ultimately, parents should look for signs that their child is interested in and capable of using the toilet before beginning toilet learning.

It is important that the child is able to wipe herself, clean, or pull down her pants when there is an urge to urinate or use the potty.

Ensure that your child's clothing is easy to put on and take off and train them to dress and undress themselves. You may distract him by providing toys, books, or coloring to entertain him while waiting for a bowel movement. Other motor skills to check are if the child is able to:

- unzip their pants.
- Pull underwear and pants up and down.
- Wipe themselves.
- Grasp objects well.

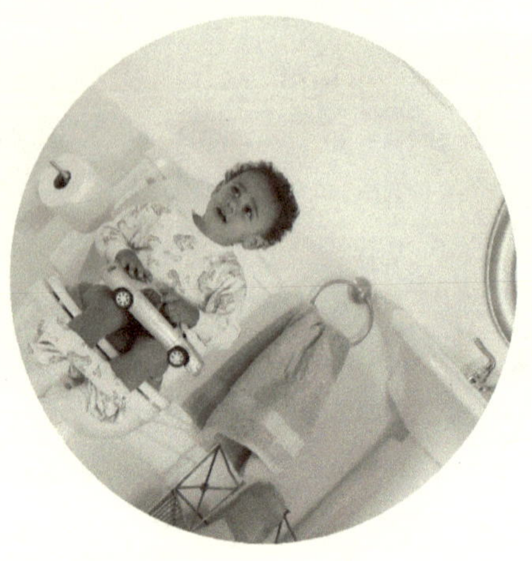

What Is Physiological Readiness?

When parents talk about their child being "ready" to toilet learn, they are usually referring to psychological readiness. This is different from physiological readiness, which refers to the physical maturity required for successful toileting.

Although there is no single indicator of psychological readiness, there are a few key signs that parents can look for. For example, most children who are ready to toilet learn will express an interest in using the toilet and will be able to follow simple instructions.

Ch. 3: Factors that Negatively Influence Toilet Learning

There are several factors that can negatively influence toilet learning. This chapter discusses some common reasons children might resist toilet learning and what you can do about it.

1. Parents' approach and attitude

Parents' attitude and actions during the toilet learning process can positively or negatively affect their children. Complaining about changing a child's diaper or showing disgust at the contents sends a negative message to the child. Despite the fact that going in the diaper is a natural, normal, and healthy process for them at this point, these attitudes can make a child feel that she is doing something wrong.

Each child learns at her own pace, and each child will be different. If parents are feeling stressed or angry about toilet learning, they will likely communicate this to their child. This can create a negative association with the potty and make the child resistant to using it.

Overly involved parents may try to force their children to use the potty. In this situation, the child may feel anxious and overwhelmed, which makes her less likely to use the potty.

Take a step back if you find yourself having these attitudes and examine the reasons behind them. It is important to remind yourself that your child is healthy and developing normally. Examine some hidden expectations from yourself or society regarding toileting.

2. Lack of an Example for the Child

A child may ask why she needs to use a potty if she is already doing fine with her diapers or pants on. It probably hasn't even occurred to her that other kids might be using a potty. It’s important to demonstrate the use of a potty to the child in order for him to see how it's done.

Your child might be too shy or embarrassed to use the potty. She may be afraid of getting wet and messy when she goes potty, so she may not want to get into the habit of using it.

He might not understand what it means to sit on the toilet. Again, this is where demonstrating to your child how to use the potty or toilet is important. Explain to your child what you are doing and get them involved by letting them try to imitate you.

Seeing a parent use the toilet can help alleviate many of the issues mentioned and help your child become comfortable with toilct learning.

3. The Child Is Not Ready for Toilet Learning

Toilet learning is a process, not an event. It takes time to develop a strong bladder and bowel control. Wait until your child is older and more confident with her bladder control before starting this process or give yourself a little extra time before trying to assist your child with toilet learning.

4. Child Has Issues with Constipation

It is important to know that children who experience constipation frequently often have difficulty with toilet learning. It is not something that should be ignored. Consult her doctor if your child is experiencing frequent constipation. They can help determine what might be causing the problem.

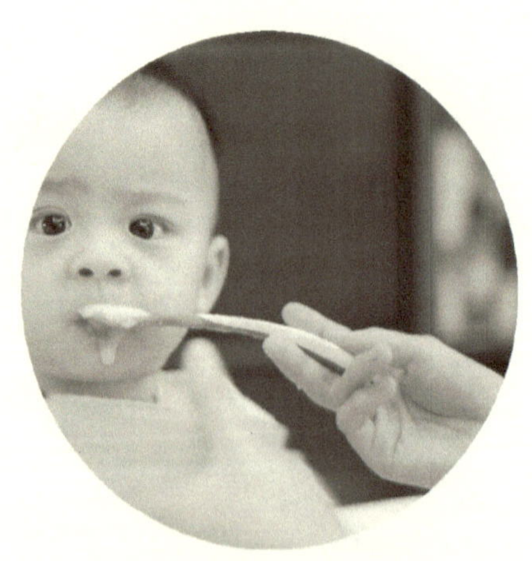

It is important to ensure that your child's diet is as healthy as possible. Include plenty of fruits and vegetables as well as plenty of water. This will prevent constipation and facilitate their toilet learning process.

5. Using Pull-Ups

I'm sure you have seen the advertisement for pull-ups, colorful with fun characters. They give parents and caregivers the impression that their child is on the way from diapers to toilet learning, but that is an illusion. They may be appealing but they cannot change the fact a child has to be physiologically and psychologically ready.

Pull-ups are garments that may help a child feel like she no longer needs to wear a baby diaper. However, pull-ups remove two key factors that motivate a child to learn to use a toilet: not wanting to feel wet and wanting to be like big kids. Pull-ups might be great for companies since they are more expensive than diapers, but they don't help the toilet learning process. Instead, the use of pull-ups prolongs the process.

Ch. 4. When Not to Start Toilet Learning

While toilet learning is an important developmental milestone, there are certain circumstances when it may be best to delay starting the process:

1. If your child is not showing signs of readiness: Every child develops at his/her own pace, so it's important to wait until your child is showing signs of readiness before starting toilet learning. Some signs of readiness include being able to stay dry for longer periods, showing an interest in using the toilet, and being able to follow simple instructions.
2. During times of stress or major life changes: Toilet learning can be stressful for both parents and children, so it's best to avoid starting the process during times of stress or major life changes, such as moving to a new home or the arrival of a new sibling.
3. If your child is experiencing any physical or emotional difficulties: If your child is experiencing physical or emotional difficulties, such as constipation or anxiety, it may be best

to delay starting toilet learning until those issues have been addressed.

4. If your family is not ready: Toilet learning requires patience, consistency, and a willingness to provide lots of encouragement to your child. If your family is not ready to commit to the process, it may be best to delay starting until everyone is on board.

In general, it's important to remember that every child is unique and there is no "right" age for toilet learning. The key is to be patient, flexible, and responsive to your child's needs and development.

How to start toilet learning

Toilet learning is an important milestone for children as they move toward greater independence and self-care. Here are some general tips on how to start toilet learning:

- Look for readiness signs: Before starting toilet learning, observe your child for signs of readiness. These signs may include showing an interest in the bathroom or in wearing underwear, telling you when they need to go, staying dry for longer periods of time, or having regular bowel movements.
- Introduce the potty: Introduce your child to the potty chair and let them explore it. Encourage them to sit on it, fully clothed, and explain what it's for. You may want to let them decorate it with stickers or let them pick out a special potty chair.
- Make it a routine: Set up a routine for sitting on the potty chair, such as after meals or when they wake up from a nap. Consistency is key, so try to stick to the routine as much as possible.

- Be patient: Toilet learning can be frustrating for both you and your child, so be patient and don't get discouraged if progress is slow. Every child is different and will learn at their own pace.

Remember that toilet learning is a process, and it may take some time before your child is fully comfortable using the potty. With patience, consistency, and a positive attitude, your child will eventually master using the toilet.

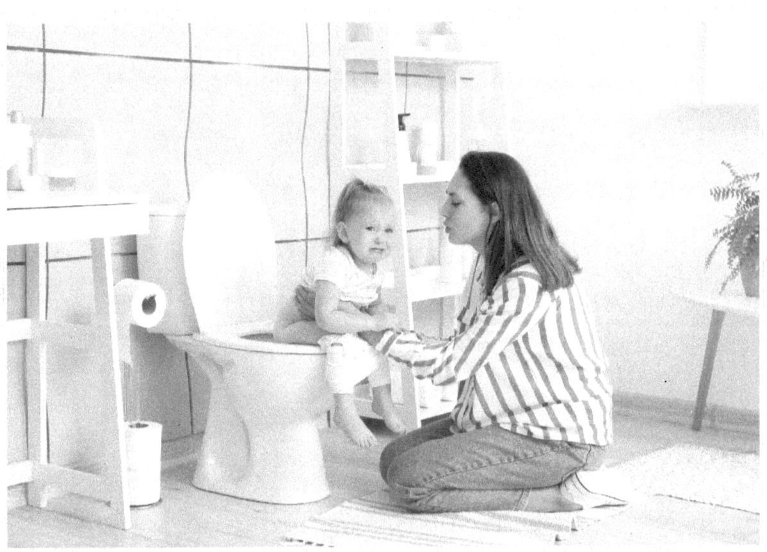

Moving From Diapers to Underwear

There is no one-size-fits-all when it comes to toilet learning. Depending on the child, some may be ready as early as 18 months of age, while others may not be ready until they are three years old. The most important thing is to wait until your child shows signs that she is ready to start toilet learning.

The transition from diapers to underwear is an exciting milestone for parents and children. For children, it marks a major step towards independence and self-care. For parents, it can be a welcome relief from the daily task of changing diapers. To help make the transition as smooth as possible, there are a few things to remember.

- First, it is important to involve your child in the process. Explain why you are making the switch from diapers to underwear and let her choose her own pair of underwear.

- Secondly, start with small steps. Allow your child to wear his underwear for short periods of time at first, gradually increasing the amount of time he spends in them each day.
- Finally, be prepared for accidents. It is inevitable that there will be a few accidents along the way. Just remember to stay positive and encourage your child throughout the process. With a little patience and understanding, you will soon be able to say goodbye to diapers for good.

Once you have decided to start, there are a few things you can do to make the process go more smoothly. A positive attitude and lots of patience are the most essential. It's also helpful to come up with a plan and stick to it. Always encourage your child whenever accidents occur.

Choosing the Right Potty Seat for Your Child

Every child is unique, as we mentioned earlier. While some are ready to take the plunge at an early age, others need a little more time. One thing that all children have in common is the need for a potty seat that is both comfortable and safe. With so many options on the market, it can take time to figure out where to start.

Here are a few things to keep in mind when choosing the right potty seat for your child:

- Consider your child's age and stage of development- younger children will need a potty seat with a higher backrest and sides that provide support and stability.
- Level of comfort- Some children prefer a potty seat with a soft, padded surface, while others find that a smooth plastic seat is more comfortable. Consider features like armrests or a built-in footrest.

- Safety- this is always a priority when choosing a potty seat. Look for seats with nonslip surfaces and sturdy construction.

How to Make Toilet Learning Fun!

No one likes change, least of all toddlers. That's why it's important to make toilet learning as fun and stress-free as possible for both you and your child.

Here are a few tips:

- Buy your child a special "potty seat" or "toilet seat cover" that they can use just for them. This will make them feel grown up and special.
- Let them pick out their own "big kid" underwear. Wearing fun character underwear will make them want to keep them clean!

- Make it educational and let them have an adorable “little buddy” that will help your child feel more comfortable using the potty. This will help them feel like they're not alone in their new skill, and it'll encourage them to keep practicing until they get it right.
- Give your child permission to take breaks during toilet learning so they can get things done, then come back and try again later.
- Create a positive atmosphere where you can feel safe talking about toilet learning. Gently encourage your child by using positive reinforcement such as saying, "I'm proud of you!" or "You did good!"

Toilet learning is a rite of passage for little ones. It's a time when kids learn to make the transition from diapers to big kid pants. So be prepared for both excitement and nerves!

Diet and Hydration While Toilet Learning

It's vital to ensure that your child is well-hydrated with lots of water to keep their bowels functioning well. Encourage her to take foods that are rich in fiber. Fiber helps the body maintain normal bowel movements and keeps the digestive system working properly. Ensure your child does not skip meals or eat too much in one sitting to avoid constipation.

Some foods that are high in fiber include:

- Berries- A cup serving contains eight grams of fiber.
- Apples- Contains water and fiber.

- High-fiber wheat bread - This specific bread provides a variety of minerals, including iron, magnesium, and B vitamins. It will also aid in regular bowel movements.
- Oranges- citrus fruits contain lots of vitamins and fiber. This is beneficial during toilet learning, especially with children that have diarrhea.
- Others include brussels sprouts, leafy vegetables, legumes, oats, nuts, sweet potatoes, and high-fiber yogurts.

Tips for Transitioning from a Potty Seat to Using the Toilet

When your child shows interest in using the toilet and you don't need to toilet train at night, it's time to transition from potty to toilet. Your child will benefit from this whenever he or she is in school or traveling.

Here are some tips to help when transitioning your toddler:

- Start by letting your child sit on the toilet with their clothes on. This will help them get used to the new environment
- Show them how to use the toilet i.e. how to flush and let them try
- Make the required adjustments such as adding a stepping stool for easier access
- Transition them gradually
- Encourage them to urinate frequently, even if they don't have to go. This will help train their body to associate the urge to urinate with using the toilet.
-

- Make sure they understand how to properly wipe themselves after going. Help them practice if necessary.
- Praise them whenever they use the toilet successfully. This positive reinforcement will help motivate them to keep up the good work.

Ch. 5: Teaching the Toileting Process

A crucial developmental stage for your child is learning how to use the bathroom. While some toddlers pick it up quickly, others require parental help and patience.

Don't begin toilet learning too soon. Typically, it takes children until they are 18 months to two years old before they can recognize and act on urination cues like a full bladder. Early toilet training can make your child sad. You might also become annoyed and frustrated since the child may not do as you ask them to.

Before a youngster can consistently keep their bed dry at night, they often have mastered daytime toileting. You can try a lot of doable tips to control bedwetting. Adding a nightlight in the bathroom or hallway might solve your problems quickly!

Create a routine. Have your child use the restroom at specific times during the day, such as right after meals or snacks, before and after naps, and before going to bed.

- Assist your child in acquiring toilet habits. Allow them to use the potty while dressed, and then prod them to use it for a short period of time without a diaper.
- Watch for indications that they need to visit the restroom. Remind your child to let you know when they need to go. Even if they inform you after the fact, make sure to give them praise.
- Boys typically start learning to urinate while seated. This is all right. They can pick up how to stand afterward.
- While using the toilet, reading to your child may help them unwind.
- Teach your child to wash his or her hands after using the restroom.
- Encourage your child to try cotton underwear or training pants if they have successfully used the potty for at least a week. Make this a memorable occasion.

Wiping

- Teach your youngster the appropriate way to wipe. When wiping, girls should go from front to back. Most will require your help wiping until they are preschoolers, especially after bowel movements.
- Display the appropriate method. The potty-training method has to continue to emphasize this crucial milestone.
- Teach your child to hold the wipe in their hand flat (not wadded into a ball). and then guide them through the wipe, fold, wipe, fold, wipe process until there is nothing left on the wipe. They'll be able to flush after they're done using it that way.

Practice Makes Perfect

- Have your child attempt to wipe themselves clean after using the toilet each time, before assisting them in cleaning themselves up.

- Try having them practice going to the toilet when you aren't around so that they learn how to be alone in their bathroom.
- You should also try giving them more opportunities to use the toilet at home, for instance, by setting aside part of one bathroom as their own.

Hand Hygiene

Utilize a sturdy footstool to make your sink area kid-friendly by allowing children to easily reach the water and sink. Lower necessary objects (soap, towels, wipes) to your child's level. Use soft towels and unscented soaps according to your child's sensory demands, and make sure the water's temperature is "nice to go."

Show and walk them through each process as you demonstrate and instruct them. Let them witness you turn on the water, wet your hands, apply soap, wash, rinse, and then dry them.

Try a new kind of soap if one doesn't work or if your child doesn't like one. Soap comes in foam, gel, a bar, liquid, scented, unscented, small personal-size bars, and textured bars of soap.

The process might become "fun" for your youngster if you use colored and color-changing soaps (foamy, gels, pens). To help them understand the procedure and the specifics, assist them as required while letting them do as much of it on their own. Create "dots" or "lines" on your child's hands with kid-safe water-soluble markers or paint, then have them wash them off. Start with only one mark to gauge your child's reaction.

Night Dryness

Ensure that your child can simply get out of bed and take off their pajamas. Encourage your child to lift them up and down on their own.

Talk to your child about using the bathroom after dark. Together, determine your procedure. Will they wake you up for assistance, use a potty in their bedroom, or go to the bathroom independently?

You might need to discuss your preferred nighttime toileting method several times. You may say, "come into my bedroom and wake me up when you need to use the restroom, and I'll help you," for instance.

Place a waterproof mattress covering over their mattress. Make sure your child can see well enough and has easy access to the bathroom at night by using a nightlight as mentioned earlier.

Accidents Will Happen

Accidents are most likely to happen when children are embarrassed or ashamed, upset or frightened, overly excited or overly tired, in a strange place, changing their routine, ill, having problems or disturbances at home, or so busy playing they forget.

Children often urinate more frequently on rainy days or when the weather is cold.

Be understanding of accidents and regressions as you would be in any other learning experience. Never shame, scold, or punish a child for an accident or a regression.

Reassure your child with comforting words like these:

"you're learning .it takes time."

"Accidents happen, and that's okay."

"I'm sure you forgot because you were busy playing with your fun toy. It's okay. Next time, you will probably remember."

As children go through the day's activities, be sure to give them potty breaks.

When Problems Occur

Physical health problems can hinder toilet learning progress. Before beginning toilet learning, parents may need to consult the child's pediatrician to determine if the child has a medical condition that might interfere with toilet learning success. Any gastrointestinal issues, such as diarrhea or constipation, should be addressed.

The child should drink plenty of water and get plenty of fiber to prevent constipation. The experience of a painful bowel movement may seriously interfere with a child's progress.

Recognition

Offering children rewards like stickers, candy, etc., is not a positive practice. What you are teaching a child is to expect a tangible reward for doing something she or he is supposed to do. For children, the accomplishment itself, in this case, being able to poop or pee in a toilet is a very meaningful reward to them. Just recognition for learning to go to the toilet, but not over-praise is enough. Over-praising can make a child feel like a failure when the next time she or he is not successful.

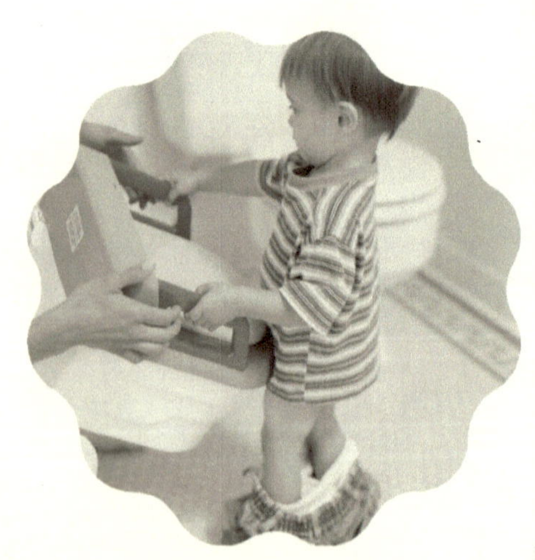

Ch.6: Toilet Learning for Children with Special Needs

Toilet learning for a child with special needs can be a frustrating experience. However, there are some basic steps you can take to make the process easier and more successful.

Children with special needs are often more sensitive to the environment around them and more easily frustrated by their inability to communicate what they need. This can lead to delayed toilet learning, along with other issues such as bedwetting or constipation.

A child with special needs may have trouble learning how to control their bladder and bowel movements. They may also be physically unable to hold down a bowel movement, or they might be unable to feel when they need to go. This can make it difficult for them to tell their body that they are ready to go.

You might have to check with a doctor/expert/parents of other special needs children. The readiness for special needs children are similar to those for other children. Your child may have some disabilities or health issues that could affect their ability to learn how to use the toilet. Some children with disabilities may not even be able to communicate their need for toileting until they have had a chance to learn how to communicate through speech and language therapy.

You should also consider their age and developmental level when deciding how much time you'll spend on toilet learning.

However, it is recommended that you seek the advice of a pediatrician to determine how much the training process is affected, any special needs that the child may require during training, and any special equipment needed.

Before you and your child start the process, it's crucial to mentally and emotionally prepare yourself. You need to be aware of the fact that children with special needs usually start toilet training later than other children and the process is slower and takes longer in most cases. These children will also require to be constantly assisted in all aspects while toilet learning. Therefore, as a parent, you need to be extra patient with your special needs child.

Examples of these challenges include:

Physical Conditions

Physical challenges can affect a child with special needs to toilet learn. The child may be affected by an illness or other physical disabilities that make it difficult for them to learn how to use the toilet. For example, they may have trouble sitting down and holding it until they feel the urge to go; they may not be able to reach certain parts of the toilet, or they may not have enough strength in their legs to stand up from sitting on the toilet. You need to consider any physical challenges that might affect the child's ability to use the toilet and work with those challenges in order to make sure that the child can successfully complete toilet learning.

Children with Hearing Difficulties

Toilet learning may or may not be difficult for children who are deaf or have hearing impairments, depending on how well they can communicate. You should use signs and gestures to communicate, and the child is able to learn through a combination of visual observation and your explanations. Toilet learning may need to wait till a child is a little older if they are unable to comprehend your signals and simple signs.

Keep the learning process straightforward and you may also use illustrations such as showing them pictures of the same and letting them watch other children using the bathroom. Use gestures that the child is able to understand and be able to use as well. After successful training, praise your child to motivate them to keep up.

Blindness and Visual Difficulties

Children with severe vision impairments do not use the essential visual aids and cues, such as toilet-themed picture books and watching parents and siblings use the restroom, so they cannot imitate their actions. This is a big disadvantage to them as they are unable to locate the potty in the bathroom, see how urine and feces enter the potty, and how one tears off and uses toilet paper. These kids most often train later than children without vision impairments because they rely more on cognitive and linguistic abilities.

Initial assistance and supervision with the toileting process are important and the child needs assistance with activities such as how to sit on the toilet, pulling pants down, using toilet paper, washing hands after, and general toilet exploration.

It is crucial to keep the tiny potty in the same location in the bathroom so that the child can always find it. A small potty on the floor is likely to be more accessible than a potty seat on the adult toilet. Your child will also have to rely more on language to comprehend how the process works without sight to aid them.

Since language impairments can accompany blindness, you should usually wait until your child is three or four years old (or even later) to start toilet learning so that they can fully understand what you are saying to them. Also, keep the way free of obstacles so that the child can easily access the toilet area.

Cerebral palsy

Toilet learning may be more difficult for children with cerebral palsy due to their physical restrictions, and much patience and persistence are required to assist them during the learning process.

Since cerebral palsy is a disability that ranges from mild to severe, consult with your child's pediatrician to guide you on the proper steps to follow. Studies have also shown that children with cerebral palsy have a slower rate of bladder development, and they might not have enough bladder awareness at two to three years to start training.

Therefore, they will need more assistance in understanding when to use the bathroom, including fidgeting, grasping genitals, etc. Some with cerebral palsy will be able to communicate their need for the bathroom, but they may require your assistance in taking off their clothes or your support until they can do it independently. Guide them on how to hold off urination, take off clothes and be able to sit through the toilet process.

Diet is also important to pay close attention to. This is due to the fact that children with cerebral palsy will easily experience constipation due to less exercise, underdeveloped muscle tone, or medication. Ensure to feed them with high-fiber foods such as fruits and vegetables as discussed above. Also, provide enough fluids for hydration and bowel movements.

Autism

Children with autism spectrum disorder (ASD) can take a little longer to learn many activities including how to use the potty. At least 50% of kids with autism spectrum disorders are cognitively impaired, which affects about 1 in 150 children. It is likely that these children will have difficulty using language, making social connections, and repeating behaviors.

Many children with ASD take longer to figure out how to use the bathroom. They tend to start using the restroom much later in life, due to a few typical issues they encounter. As parents or caregivers, understanding these issues can enable you to think of new solutions to satisfy your child's requirements.

The child may have difficulty understanding the language, pulling their pants down, be afraid of toilets flushing, may not be aware that the clothes are soiled, or getting used to a toileting routine.

If a child with autism is non-verbal, they will need to use different means of communication including pictures or sign language to communicate to you the need to use the restroom. Promote autonomy to your child so that they can be free to lead the toilet learning process.

Some tips to help you deal with autism include:

- Stay positive and encourage your child
- Support your child's communication with nonverbal methods
- Allow your child to self-regulate in behaviors like flapping the hands or spinning in circles, as a means of self-regulation.

Acknowledge that their behavior is a way of communicating.

Consult and have sessions with an autism specialist on child-specific toilet learning obstacles, early behavioral indicators that a child is ready to transition, use of adaptive supports, and reinforcement techniques for successful training.

Spinal Injury

Children with neurogenic bladder brought on by spina bifida, spinal cord injury, or tumors have similar toilet training issues to those affected by cerebral palsy or any other illness. These children do not acquire sufficient bladder awareness to urinate at the toilet and the right time to visit the bathroom.

However, you can train your child to self-catheterize to manage to remove urine on a regular basis and visit the bathroom regularly for bowel movements.

Developmental Delays

Children who have communicative and cognitive disabilities delay in showing readiness signs as opposed to children that do not have delays. The toilet learning process usually gets simpler as the child develops basic level of verbal ability, is able to dress themselves, pull down their pants, wash hands, and exhibits awareness of the need to relieve themselves. Some of these abilities can be taught to children before they are able to control and be conscious of their bladders. Seek consultation and work with a speech-language therapist to improve functional communication abilities to make the process easy.

It is best to train your child with developmental delays in small steps such as letting them watch and observe while you or other children use the restroom, then learn slowly how to use, wipe themselves and clean up after. Stay positive and motivated to accomplish this.

Incontinence

The term incontinence refers to the inability to control one's pee or bowel movements voluntarily. While some children take just weeks to master bladder and bowel control, others struggle for years. A child can experience incontinence during the daytime, night, or both. Children are not regarded to have daytime incontinence until they are 5 or older or nighttime incontinence until they are at least 7 years old because all children are different, and some take longer than others to train to use the bathroom.

Incontinence may be caused by issues such as:

- Medical disorders, including diabetes and urinary tract infections (UTIs),
- Constipation
- Anatomical anomalies, such as spina bifida or issues with the spinal cord
- Stress from emotions
- Improper urination posture
- Sexual assault
- A diet that includes acidic drinks and caffeine
- Having infrequent urination
-

Bedwetting refers to nighttime incontinence and can be caused by:

- Early bladder contraction
- Developmental delay
- Bedwetting in the family history
- Deep sleeping
- Taking excessive fluids just before bedtime

Setting up a regular potty schedule for your child is the best way to resolve this situation. Ensure frequent toilet visits if they take in too much fluids and also remind them after every hour or two to use the bathroom.

Other Behavioral Difficulties

Other difficulties that may affect toilet learning include oppositional defiant disorder (ODD), fetal alcohol syndrome (FAS), and attention-deficit/hyperactivity disorder (ADHD). Most of the children affected by these behavioral difficulties may be less motivated to respond to positive reinforcements that work well with other children. It may be more difficult to toilet-train the child with such issues.

Because formal diagnoses (such as attention-deficit/hyperactivity disorder or oppositional defiant disorder) are typically not given until the preschool years or later, parents and caregivers of these children frequently struggle to receive professional support.

You should learn more about your child's strengths, challenges, tendencies, and interests for the process to run smoothly. Many children with behavioral difficulties may find it challenging to adapt to any change and will get sensitive to new environments, some will not want to be touched and will often feel upset by these factors.

It is very crucial to adjust the goals for a toilet learning program to the child's existing aptitude.

The majority of children with special needs can be trained to use the toilet, despite obstacles, whether they have physical impairments or behavioral problems. However, in certain situations, the procedure may take up to a year or even longer. Always consult with a physical therapist, to assist in ensuring the process is a successful one.

Ch. 7: Conclusion

Learning to use the potty is a challenge, but it's an important part of growing up. Knowing when it's time to start toilet learning, and how to help your child achieve success will make the process smoother. It takes patience and understanding to teach the child to show respect for the body and how to care for it. They need instruction on how to use the toilet as well as when to call for help when things get stuck. Toilet learning is a process that parents and children should enjoy together. Some children learn quickly, while others take longer, but it's all part of the learning process.

Parents and caregivers need to stay positive, and patient, and support the child through this major milestone. Toilet learning can be done in a few days, a week, or later in childhood. Pick what works for you and your child and enjoy the experience.

Immaculate Newsted is a blogger, children's book author, and licensed Daycare provider. She has worked with younger children for nearly two decades as a childcare provider which is why she was inspired to write this potty-training book. She lives in Maryland with her husband and their three beautiful children.
To learn more about her work please visit https://gracedisshe.com and follow her on social media.

About the Editor

Dr. Alice Koech is a writer, editor, course creator, and coach. She writes on topics including personal development, mental health, mindset, and parenting. You can find her online at www.Koechconsulting.com or on social media at @dr.alicekoech (Instagram).

want to learn more?

sign up!

www.ingramcontent.com/pod-product-compliance
Lightning Source LLC
LaVergne TN
LVHW050943080826
845145LV00004B/1392

* 9 7 8 1 9 5 4 6 8 2 5 5 9 *